Better Together
Two-Block Designs for Dynamic Quilts

Karen Sievert

Better Together: Two-Block Designs
for Dynamic Quilts
© 2010 by Karen Sievert

That Patchwork Place® is an imprint
of Martingale & Company®.

Martingale & Company
20205 144th Ave. NE
Woodinville, WA 98072-8478 USA
www.martingale-pub.com

Printed in China
15 14 13 12 11 10   8 7 6 5 4 3 2 1

**Library of Congress Cataloging-in-Publication Data
is available upon request.**

ISBN: 978-1-56477-938-0

Dedication

*To my husband, Vince. As my rock,
you've kept me grounded. As my
wings, you've encouraged me to soar
and reach for the stars. As my crutch,
you've given me someone to always
lean on. As my love, you've constantly
fulfilled me. No wife could ask for
more, and I will always be thankful
for your presence in my life. I love
you, now and always.*

Mission Statement

*Dedicated to providing quality products
and service to inspire creativity.*

Credits

President & CEO: Tom Wierzbicki
Editor in Chief: Mary V. Green
Managing Editor: Tina Cook
Developmental Editor: Karen Costello Soltys
Technical Editor: Laurie Baker
Copy Editor: Sheila Chapman Ryan
Design Director: Stan Green
Production Manager: Regina Girard
Illustrator: Laurel Strand
Cover & Text Designer: Adrienne Smitke
Photographer: Brent Kane

Acknowledgments

No man, or woman, is an island! I certainly couldn't have done this without the love and support of a few key people.

❀ First, my husband, Vince. You kept telling me (for a couple of years) I should write a book. I definitely have to thank you for believing in me, even when I didn't fully believe in myself. Your continual love and support have been necessary throughout this process, and I can truly say this would never have happened without you!

❀ To my children: Wayne, Shannah, and Travis. Thanks for picking up the slack! I know I don't tell you often enough, but I'm so proud of each of you. You're the greatest! Love you all!

❀ To my mother, Marlene Johnson. I think all children flourish with a mother's love, regardless of their age. Thanks, Mom, for always believing in me, encouraging me, and picking me up when I fall. I love you so much!

❀ My mother-in-law, Jennie Miles. Did I hit the jackpot or what? You're the best mom-in-law a girl could ever hope to have. I respect and admire you, and am so proud to call you "Mom." Love you!

❀ My sister, Barbara. You got me started on this crazy journey by dragging me into that quilt shop! Thank you!

❀ Phyllis Marshall, my longtime friend. Remember when we first met? Such a long time ago, yet, you're always there for me—to encourage, to listen, to laugh (and cry), and just about anything else! Thanks; I love you!

❀ Martha Williams, another very wonderful friend. Thank you more than I can say for all your help. Sewing, binding, whatever I needed; you were there! Thank you ever so much!

Midnight Fairy Lights

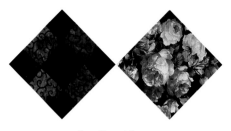

Sun-Kissed Roses

Sherbet Stars

Contrasting Stars

Roman Tile

Star Flower

Framing the Stars

Sew Dear

Circles, Stars, and Medallions

Stacie's Quilt

Contents

Introduction 7

Fabric 8

Quiltmaking Basics 10

The Patterns

Midnight Fairy Lights 17

Sun-Kissed Roses 20

Sherbet Stars 23

Contrasting Stars 27

Roman Tile 32

Star Flower 38

Framing the Stars 43

Sew Dear 48

Circles, Stars, and Medallions 52

Stacie's Quilt 56

About the Author 63

Introduction

Have you ever noticed how some things are just, well, better together? Each item can be great individually, but the magic occurs in the joining. Like a stained-glass window: it's beautiful on its own yet truly magical when the sun pours through it, giving it a luminosity that was unappreciated before!

Better Together is like that stained-glass window. This is a book about one- and two-block quilt patterns: individually beautiful, but absolutely stunning when joined! The patterns range in complexity; some are easy enough for the beginning quilter and some are better for the intermediate quilter. What they have in common, though, is their natural charm and elegance, making quilters of all skill levels eager to make them.

I believe that quiltmaking is a journey; at least, it has been for me! As you go through the quilts in this book, you'll develop skills that help you to easily accomplish the more complex patterns. And if you're unsure about any of the skills needed to make your trip successful, there are sections in the book that were written to help guide you. Are you having problems choosing fabric? The chapter on fabric (page 8) will give you insight as to how I choose fabrics. I even show you a way to cheat if you're having problems! In "Quiltmaking Basics" on page 10, we'll cover topics such as rotary cutting,

piecing, and pinning. And I'll share with you my favorite techniques for borders and binding. Whether you're a new quilter or one well established in the skills of quiltmaking, this section can provide valuable insight. I'm always learning from others, and I enjoy trying out different techniques. If it's faster, easier, or more accurate, I'm there!

The patterns begin on page 17. Have a blast with "Sun-Kissed Roses" on page 20, a quilt you can make in a day. Be enchanted with the blended look of "Sherbet Stars" on page 23. And think of a friend or two as you put together "Sew Dear" on page 48. Those are just a few of the quilts you'll enjoy piecing and quilting. While I had fun designing these quilts, their true beauty was revealed in the making.

I sincerely hope you'll enjoy the patterns as much as I have, and that the quilts you make bring you years of comfort and a wealth of smiles. And my wish is that *your* quiltmaking journey is as fondly remembered as mine. I feel so blessed with quilting. Not only has it given me a wonderful creative outlet, it's also given me some of the best friends in the world! It makes me realize that we are all *better together*!

God bless you, your families, and, yes, your quilts!

~Karen

Fabric

Fabric is the heart and soul of every quilt. It is the beautiful beginning of each project. It's what gets me excited, motivates me to create, and sustains me as I work. It's why I can't wait to see the finished product. Truly, what would a quilt be without fabric?

This chapter is dedicated to selecting and preparing your fabrics, both of which are crucial to our success. I believe the tips you receive here will help you with your own creations, making them heirlooms you can treasure year after year.

Fabric Selection

Wow! When I first started quilting, fabric selection was the hardest part for me! My sister dragged me into a quilt shop, firmly stating that I needed a hobby, and then I spent three *agonizing* hours trying to pick out fabric. The whole process felt so intimidating. Yet now, it's one of my favorite parts of quilting. With a little help, it can become your favorite part, too.

The trick for me is to find one piece, usually a print, that just sings to my soul. You know the one . . . when you walk into the quilt shop, you see the fabric, pick up the bolt, and then never put it down because you're afraid someone else might snatch it up. Don't laugh, I do that all the time! Honest.

From that one print, which I call my focus fabric, I'll pull my other colors. A neat trick is to look at the selvage of your focus fabric; printed on it will be dots of all the colors used in creating that piece. Those dots very easily tell you which colors will work with that fabric.

There are other factors I try to keep in mind as I make my selections. For instance, does the pattern have really large pieces? If so, it would be perfect for showcasing large-scale prints that you just can't bring yourself to cut up. Or does the pattern have lots of small pieces? In that case, a small-scale print would work better.

The style of the fabric can also influence your choices. It's hard to imagine a civil-war print paired with an Asian print. I'm sure it can be done; however, for me, selecting fabrics with similar styles or themes creates a

Use the selvage dye dots as a guide when coordinating fabrics.

more harmonious piece. If you select fabrics you love to look at, you'll have more fun making your quilts.

Last, but not least, I look at what I want the overall effect of the quilt to be. If I'm aiming for a "blended" look, then I want the colors, styles, and scale of prints to be complementary—to flow into each other. On the other hand, if I'm shooting for high contrast, then I'll pick fabrics that stand out from each other—colors that pop.

The bottom line is, don't be afraid to experiment. Fabric selection should be fun and exciting. This is the start of a new project—today's quilt and tomorrow's heirloom. Chances are if you love the fabric when you start, you'll enjoy making the quilt, and love it that much more when you're done!

Fabric Preparation

First of all, I *always* use 100%-cotton fabric purchased from a quality quilt shop. When I first started quilting, I tried saving money by buying fabrics from places other than quilt shops, but found, much to my dismay, that the fabrics tended to be inferior in quality. It didn't take long for me to realize that the extra pennies saved didn't matter if the fabric was falling apart!

Secondly, I *always* prewash my fabrics. I know a lot of quilters who don't prewash, but from my experience, I've found that prewashing is the right thing to do. Here's why: Fabrics shrink, and they sometimes bleed. The time to find out that a fabric bleeds is not *after* you've spent all that time cutting, piecing, and quilting. I know, because it's happened to me twice, and I was devastated that those quilts were ruined.

Before I wash my fabric, I use pinking shears to clip the corners at the selvage of the fabric. Doing this helps reduce fraying, and it also provides a visual cue that the fabric has been washed. I can always look in my stash of fabrics and tell by those clipped edges which fabrics have and have not been prewashed.

Selvages

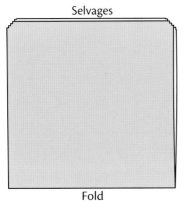

Fold

Also, again from experience, wash your dark and light fabrics separately. Every time I ignore my own advice and wash them together, well, of course, that's when a dark fabric will bleed onto a light one. There's nothing more frustrating than ruining a good piece of fabric.

Once washed, I put the fabrics in the dryer *without* a fabric softener sheet. And from there, it's off to the iron. I personally like to "resize" the fabric, so I use spray sizing or spray starch while I iron to give the fabric back some of the crispness that was lost when it was washed. I think that's why some quilters don't prewash—they don't want to lose the sizing. For me, a starched fabric is so much easier to work with, especially on those pesky bias edges. I recommend spraying the fabrics with a good quality spray starch or sizing, and then letting them rest for about 15 minutes. This allows the starch to really soak into the fibers and eliminates flaking. After the fabrics rest, I iron them on a high heat setting with steam. My iron easily handles the high heat setting, but you may want to check yours on a scrap of fabric to ensure that it doesn't scorch the fabric. Use the highest heat setting possible that removes the wrinkles yet doesn't harm the fabric.

Quiltmaking Basics

There are several skills that are vital to successful quiltmaking. As a beginner, I scoffed at the importance of these skills, and I paid for it with quilts that just weren't quite right. I'm not a perfectionist, but I do want to make the best possible quilts I can. Whether hung on a wall, gracing a bed, or used to snuggle up in, a well-made quilt will bring us years and years of joy.

In this chapter, you'll explore skills that, if mastered, will allow you to consistently make quilts you are proud of. Rotary cutting, pressing, and accurate piecing are just a few of the topics I'll touch on. As you explore this section, realize that each topic discussed shows one way of doing things. There may be other ways of accomplishing the same thing, but over the years, these are the techniques that I have found to be tried and true.

Rotary Cutting

All of the patterns in this book are designed for rotary cutting. One rule I try to remember is that accurate cutting yields much better results. If your cutting is off, your pieces won't match when you're ready to sew them. So, as the carpenter says, "Measure twice, cut once." Reverse the position of the ruler and fabric in the following instructions if you're left-handed.

Strips

1. Fold your fabric in half lengthwise, wrong sides together, with the selvages aligned. Place the fabric on your cutting mat with the folded edge toward you. Align your ruler so that one of the horizontal lines is aligned with the fabric fold and a small portion of the fabric is visible on the right-hand side of the ruler. Cut along the long right edge of the ruler. This "squares up" the fabric and straightens the edge.

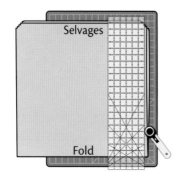

2. Rotate either the fabric or the mat so that the straightened edge is to your left. To cut strips, simply align the straightened edge with the ruler line for the desired strip. For instance, to cut 3"-wide strips, align the 3" vertical line on the ruler with the cut edge of the fabric. Once you're sure you have your ruler accurately placed and stabilized, cut along the right edge of the ruler.

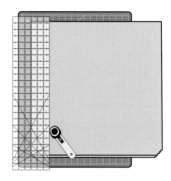

Squares and Rectangles

To cut squares and rectangles, first cut strips to the required measurement. Square up the ends of the strips in the same manner as you did for the yardage. Rotate a strip so that the squared-up edge is to your left. Measure the required distance from the straightened end and cut your piece.

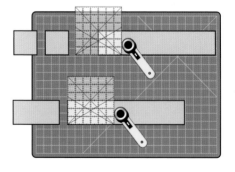

Half-Square and Quarter-Square Triangles

All of the patterns in this book use half-square and quarter-square triangles. A half-square triangle is derived from a square that has been cut diagonally once;

quarter-square triangles are derived from a square that has been cut diagonally twice.

Half-square triangles   Quarter-square triangles

Machine Piecing

OK, we've selected our fabrics, washed them, pressed them, and cut them. Now it's time to let the games begin! Using proper techniques for sewing the pieces together will ensure you love your finished project.

Accurate Seam Allowances

I can't stress enough the importance of an accurate ¼" seam allowance. I once switched sewing machines in the middle of a project and couldn't figure out why my pieces weren't fitting together properly. Turns out the ¼" foot on one machine was actually ⅜". Well, ⅛" here and ⅛" there turns into ¼" off. And as you add more pieces, the problem multiplies. So now, I *always* test my ¼" seam allowance.

Most sewing machines either come with a ¼" presser foot or the needle position can be moved to the left or right allowing you to align the edge of the presser foot with the fabric. If your machine has either of those options, test the accuracy by sewing a ¼" seam allowance. Measure to make sure it truly is ¼".

If your sewing machine doesn't have a ¼" presser foot and you can't adjust the needle position, then you'll have to mark a ¼" seam guide on the throat plate of your machine. I do this by lowering my needle onto the ¼" mark of a ruler. Then I mark the seam allowance by placing a piece of masking tape on the bed of the sewing machine next to the ruler. This gives a handy guide for aligning fabric as you're sewing.

Masking tape

Plan Ahead

One thing I like to do before sewing is to lay out all the pieces for each block in the quilt in the arrangement they will appear in the finished block. Doing this allows me to preview the fabrics I've selected and also ensures I understand where each piece goes. I refer to this arrangement as I piece each block. The few seconds it takes to do this has saved me a lot of unsewing over the years.

Pinning

To pin or not to pin? That seems to be a hotly debated question among quilters. I personally hate seam ripping, so I always pin. My girlfriend Martha never used to pin. Because she was testing patterns for me, I asked her to pin. A few days later she called me and exclaimed, "I can't believe how much better my piecing is now that I'm pinning!" Voilà, another convert.

Pinning is up to you, but keep in mind that pins hold your seams in place, which helps avoid the sewing machine's natural tendency to pull the top and bottom pieces through at different rates. I always pin abutting seams and points. I use silk pins from Clover with flat heads because they glide easily in and out of the fabric and the heads create less fabric distortion than ball heads.

Pressing, Not Ironing

There is a difference between pressing and ironing. To achieve the best possible results, you want to press, not iron.

Ironing is gliding the iron side to side and top to bottom over the fabric. This is great for clothing but not so great for patchwork because it can distort the seams and bias edges. Pressing uses the heat of the iron and not the motion. I use a hot iron without steam. Steam can also distort your seams and it will distort bias edges quicker than anything else.

Set seams by pressing them flat from the fabric wrong side. Then, open the piece and press from the right side, pressing the seam allowance in the direction indicated in the pattern. I use a straight up-and-down approach and really try hard to remember not to move the iron from side to side.

Borders

Fat, skinny, pieced, appliquéd, or plain, borders are the frame for our art. All of the quilts in this book have simple, easy-to-apply borders, yet all frame the quilts beautifully. The cutting instructions for each project indicate the number of strips to cut for the borders and the width to cut them.

Borders with Butted Corners

1. Carefully press your quilt top and lay it flat. Measure the quilt top through the vertical center.

2. Trim two border strips to the exact length measured. If necessary, join strips to obtain the measured length, and then trim the joined strip to the exact length measured.
3. Pin-mark the centers of the border strips and the sides of the quilt top.

4. With right sides together, pin the borders to the sides of the quilt top, matching centers and ends. Add more pins between the centers and ends, easing as necessary.

5. Using an accurate ¼" seam allowance, sew the borders to the sides of the quilt top. Press the seam allowances toward the border strips.
6. Once again, lay the quilt top flat. Measure the quilt top through the horizontal center, including the borders you just added.
7. Repeat steps 2–5 to attach the top and bottom borders. Press the seam allowances toward the borders.

Borders with Mitered Corners

Border strips for mitered corners must be longer than the measured width and length of the quilt top. I add double the width of the strips plus 3" to the strip length. For instance, if I'm putting on a 6"-wide border, I add 15" (6" + 6" + 3") to the strip length to ensure there is plenty of fabric to make the miter. Any excess fabric will be cut away after mitering.

1. Measure through the quilt top vertically and horizontally. Trim border strips the length as described above. Sew strips together if necessary to achieve the desired length, and then trim the joined strips to the length needed.
2. Pin-mark the center of each border strip. Divide the measurement for the quilt-top length in half. Measure this amount from the center pin on each of the side border strips and place a pin. For instance, if the quilt top measures 60", measure 30" from

the border-strip center pin and place another pin; repeat, measuring in the opposite direction from the pin. Divide the measurement for the quilt-top width in half and pin-mark the top and bottom border strips in the same manner.

3. Pin a border to the quilt top, matching centers and ensuring that the raw edges are aligned. Begin sewing ¼" in from the pinned edge, backstitching to secure, and stop sewing ¼" in from the opposite edge; backstitch. I usually mark the ¼" starting and stopping point with either a pin or pencil mark. Attach all four borders in this manner.

4. Lay the quilt-top corner that you will be mitering on an ironing board. Fold under the border strip on top at a 45° angle and align the edges with the adjacent border. Press the fold.

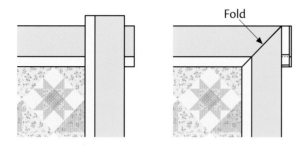
Fold

5. Fold the quilt top in half diagonally to align the horizontal and vertical borders. Pin along the pressed line to keep the strips in place, and then sew along the pressed line, beginning at the ¼" mark created when the borders were added and stitching out to the edge.

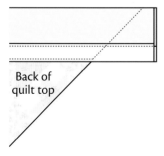
Back of quilt top

6. Trim the excess border strips ¼" away from the stitching line. Press the seam allowances open.

7. Repeat steps 4–6 for the remaining three corners.

Preparing the Quilt Sandwich

After finishing your quilt top, measure the width and length. I like my batting and backing to be 4" larger all the way around the quilt top, so add 8" to the measured width and length. This is the size that your batting and backing should measure.

1. Lay the pressed backing wrong side up on a clean, flat surface. Using masking tape, tape down the edges to prevent the backing from moving. The backing should be smooth and taut but not stretched.

2. Center the batting over the backing and smooth out any wrinkles.

3. Center the quilt top, right side up, over the batting, again smoothing out any wrinkles. Make sure to check the back of your quilt top for loose threads before laying it over the batting. They really show through, especially on light fabrics.

4. Using size 1 or 2 rustproof, curved safety pins, pin from the center out to the edges of the quilt top through all three layers. I place pins every 3" to 4". If you are hand quilting, you may want to thread baste.

Print or Plain?

Most professional quilters I know recommend using a busy print for the backing. This is so that any mistake made in the quilting process will get "lost" in the print fabric. But, a plain backing can be truly magical. If you have confidence in your quilting skills, then the back of the quilt can be almost as beautiful as the front. The choice is yours!

Quilting

Whether quilting by hand or machine, remember this maxim: Quilting makes the quilt!

Take the time to really look at your beautiful quilt top, and then decide how best to quilt it. Is an allover design best or would it look better by outline quilting your amazing patchwork? How would a quilting motif look in a large, plain square or what about using a feather motif around the border?

The actual quilting adds another design element that can greatly enhance the beauty of your quilt. Let your imagination soar so that your quilt will be one you'll cherish forever. I always look at my quilts and hope I won't say, in the future, "I wish I would have," but instead will say, "I'm so glad I did." The extra time and effort here will pay off. Today's quilts are tomorrow's heirlooms.

Binding

I love putting the binding on a quilt, simply because it means my work is almost done. After the machine binding application, I find it so rewarding and relaxing to do the final hand stitching. It gives me an opportunity to really see the beauty of what I've produced. So, let me share my favorite binding technique with you.

Preparing the Binding

1. Measure all the way around the quilt to determine the quilt perimeter. Let's say you have a quilt that is 60" x 72". You would need 264" to go around the quilt.
2. Cut enough 2"-wide selvage-to-selvage strips from your binding fabric so that when they are joined you have the required length plus an additional 10" to 12" to ensure you have plenty for mitering the corners and joining the ends. I use 2"-wide strips for binding, but you may use whatever strip width you prefer.
3. Cut both ends of your strips at a 45° angle, angling both ends in the same direction.

4. Measure ⅜" in from the tip of each strip; cut it off. Repeat on the opposite end of each strip. Doing this will help you match the ends perfectly and you won't have to trim off any dog-ears!

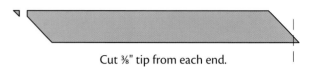

Cut ⅜" tip from each end.

5. With right sides together and ends aligned, sew the strips together to make one long strip using a ¼" seam allowance. Press the seam allowances to one side.

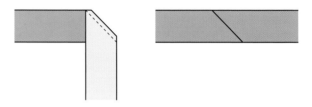

6. Press the binding strip in half lengthwise, wrong sides together.

Attaching the Binding

1. Beginning well away from the corner on one side, align the raw edges of the binding with the raw edges of the quilt. Leaving the first 10" loose, pin the binding in place.

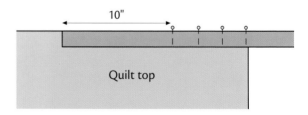

2. Using an accurate ¼" seam allowance, sew the binding to the quilt along the pinned edge. Stop ¼" from the corner and backstitch to secure.
3. Fold the binding away from the quilt so the fold makes a 45° angle.

4. With the angle still intact, bring the binding down toward the quilt and align the fold at the corner with the raw edge of the quilt.

5. Pin the binding to the next side of the quilt to be stitched. Begin sewing at the ¼" mark and sew to the next corner, remembering to stop ¼" away from the end.
6. Repeat steps 3–5 for the remaining corners.
7. After you have finished the last corner, stop sewing about 12" away from the beginning tail of the binding strip and remove the quilt from the machine.
8. Lay the quilt on a flat surface. Unfold the ends of the binding strip and lap them over each other, right sides together with the beginning binding strip end on top. With a pencil, mark where the end overlaps the underlying strip.
9. Cut through the marked strip ½" away from mark, toward the end of the strip, maintaining the 45º angle.

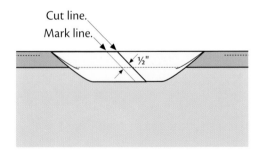

Cut line.
Mark line.
½"

10. Fold the quilt out of the way and sew the beginning and ending binding strips together using a ¼" seam allowance.
11. Refold the binding and finish stitching it to the quilt.
12. Fold the binding over the quilt raw edges and hand sew it to the back of the quilt using a blind stitch.

How to Make Freehand Feathers

As you can probably tell by looking at my quilts, I really enjoy stitching freehand feathers in my quilts. First of all, they can be very easy to create once you know the technique, and secondly, as a traditional motif they have been used in quilting practically since its inception. All feathers are not perfect in nature, and they don't have to be perfect on our quilts to still be stunning.

The technique I use is only one of many ways to quilt feathers. It's how I learned and what comes naturally to me. Feel free to put your own stamp on your feather work. That's what will make it uniquely yours.

1. Use either a chalk pencil or water-soluble marker to draw the vein of the feather onto your quilt top. Be sure you test your marking tool on a scrap of the quilt fabric to make sure the marks will come out before marking your top.

2. Using a free-motion quilting foot and with the feed dogs lowered, stitch on the marked line. When you reach the end of the line, begin stitching half-heart shapes along one side of the vein.

3. When you reach the opposite end, stitch back up along the vein of the feather, and then work your way down the opposite side of the vein with more half-heart shapes. You can stitch directly on the previous vein line or ¼" away from it to create a double vein. See, it's easy!

The beauty of freehand feathers is that they can be as unique as you are. If you like simplicity, do nothing and let the feathers speak for themselves. If you want the feathers to really pop, try stippling around them. In this example, I've personalized the feather by echo quilting around the original motif and adding vine-like tendrils, and quilting lines inside the feathers. Putting your personality into the feathers is what makes them the star of any quilt!

It may be a little intimidating at first to start stitching feather motifs on your quilt. To get over any qualms you might have, practice drawing them on paper first. I have a whole notebook filled with my attempts at drawing feathers. I drew them, and then I practiced stitching them. The more I did, the better they looked, and the more comfortable I was stitching them. Practice, practice, practice, and you too will be thrilled with your results!

Midnight Fairy Lights

Pieced and quilted by Karen Sievert

For such a simple quilt, it sure is pretty. One of the things I love most about this easy, one-block quilt is that whichever star I focus on, it seems to come forward and appear framed in black, while the others recede into the background. Then, if I look at another star, it pops forward. Pretty cool!

Finished quilt: 59½" x 59½"
Finished block: 12" x 12"

Materials

Yardages are based on 42"-wide fabric unless otherwise indicated.

3⅛ yards of black fabric for blocks, outer border, and binding
⅓ yard *each* of medium blue, medium green, and medium purple fabric for blocks
¼ yard *each* of light pink, light blue, light green, and light purple fabric for blocks
⅔ yard of fairy print for blocks
⅝ yard of medium pink fabric for blocks and inner border
2 yards of 90"-wide fabric for backing
68" x 68" piece of batting

Cutting

All measurements include ¼"-wide seam allowances.

From *each* of the medium-value fabrics, cut:

1 strip, 4¼" x 42"; crosscut into 8 squares, 4¼" x 4¼". Cut each square into quarters diagonally to yield 32 triangles (128 total).
1 strip, 3⅞" x 42"; crosscut into 8 squares, 3⅞" x 3⅞" (32 total)

From the black fabric, cut:

4 strips, 7¼" x 42"; crosscut into 16 squares, 7¼" x 7¼". Cut each square into quarters diagonally to yield 64 triangles.
4 strips, 3⅞" x 42"; crosscut into 32 squares, 3⅞" x 3⅞"
8 strips, 5½" x 42"
7 strips, 2" x 42"

From *each* of the light-value fabrics, cut:

1 strip, 4¼" x 42"; crosscut into 8 squares, 4¼" x 4¼". Cut each square into quarters diagonally to yield 32 triangles (128 total).

From the fairy print, cut:

3 strips, 6½" x 42"; crosscut into 16 squares, 6½" x 6½"

From the remainder of the medium pink, cut:

8 strips, 1" x 42"

Piecing the Blocks

1. Draw a diagonal line from corner to corner on the wrong sides of each medium-value 3⅞" square. With the marked squares on top, layer each square with a black 3⅞" square, right sides together. Stitch ¼" away from both sides of the drawn line. Cut the squares apart on the line to yield 64 half-square-triangle units (16 of each color). Press the seam allowances toward the black triangles. Trim the dog-ears.

Make 16 of each color.

2. Sew each light-value triangle to a medium-value triangle as shown to make a pieced triangle, reversing the direction of the triangles on half of the units.

Press the seam allowances toward the medium-value triangles.

Make 16 of each color.

Make 16 of each color.

3. Join a pieced triangle and a reversed pieced triangle of the same color to the short edges of each black triangle. Press the seam allowances toward the pieced triangles.

Make 16 of each color.

4. Using pieces from the same color family, lay out four units from step 1, four units from step 3, and a fairy print square into three horizontal rows. Sew the pieces in each row together. Press the seam allowances in the directions indicated. Sew the rows together. Press the seam allowances toward the middle row. Repeat to make four blocks of each color.

Make 4 of each color.

Assembling the Quilt Top

1. Refer to the quilt assembly diagram to lay out the blocks in four rows of four blocks each, arranging the colors in a pleasing manner. Sew the blocks in each row together. Press the seam allowances in opposite directions from row to row. Sew the rows together. Press the seam allowances in one direction.

2. Join two medium pink 1"-wide strips together end to end to make one long strip. Repeat to make a total of four pieced strips. Join two black 5½"-wide strips together end to end to make one long strip. Repeat to make a total of four pieced strips.

3. Refer to "Borders" on page 12 to apply the pink inner border, and then the black outer border using either the butted- or mitered-corners technique.

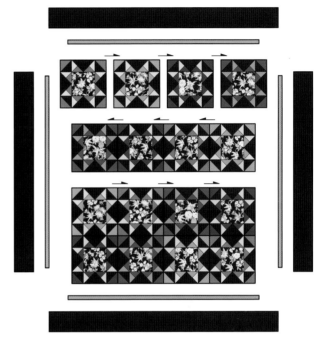

Quilt assembly

Quilting and Binding

1. Refer to "Preparing the Quilt Sandwich" on page 13 to layer the quilt top, batting, and backing.

2. Hand or machine quilt as desired.

3. Refer to "Binding" on page 14 to bind the quilt edges with the black 2"-wide strips.

Quilting Suggestion

This is a quilt where a very simple quilting style can really enhance the quilt. I outline quilted all of the elements in the blocks, crosshatched the large black squares, and did a freehand meandering floral and feather design in the border. Simple, but still spectacular!

Sun-Kissed Roses

Designed and quilted by Karen Sievert. Pieced by Martha Williams.

This quilt pairs two blocks, Nine Patch and Elongated Rail Fence, to create a sashing that is perfect for using with those large-scale prints you can't bring yourself to cut up. This is the only quilt in this book where the pieced blocks are not the focal point, but you can see how effectively the pieced blocks are used to frame the larger plain blocks. This is an easy quilt that can be stitched up in just a day, so unearth that large-scale print you've been saving for just the right project and have fun!

Finished quilt: 60½" x 60½"
Finished Plain block: 9" x 9"
Finished Nine Patch block: 3" x 3"
Finished Elongated Rail Fence block: 3" x 9"

Materials

Yardages are based on 42"-wide fabric unless otherwise indicated.

1¾ yards of black fabric for sashing blocks and outer border
1¾ yards of red print for sashing blocks, inner border, and binding
1⅝ yards of large-scale floral for Plain blocks and setting triangles
2 yards of 90"-wide fabric for backing
69" x 69" piece of batting

Cutting

All measurements include ¼"-wide seam allowances.

From the red print, cut:
22 strips, 1½" x 42"
8 strips, 1" x 42"
7 strips, 2" x 42"

From the black fabric, cut:
14 strips, 1½" x 42"
8 strips, 4½" x 42"

From the large-scale floral, cut:
4 strips, 9½" x 42"; crosscut into 13 squares, 9½" x 9½"
2 squares, 14" x 14"; cut into quarters diagonally to yield 8 triangles
2 squares, 7¼" x 7¼"; cut in half diagonally to yield 4 triangles

Piecing the Sashing Blocks and Units

1. Sew red 1½" x 42" strips to both long edges of a black 1½" x 42" strip to make strip set A. Repeat to make a total of nine strip sets. Press the seam allowances toward the black strips. Crosscut the strip sets into 36 segments, 9½" wide, for the Elongated Rail Fence blocks.

9½"

Strip set A.
Make 9. Cut 36 segments.

2. Using the 1½" x 42" strips, sew black strips to both long edges of a red print strip to make strip set B. Repeat to make a total of two strip sets. Sew the two remaining red print strips to both long edges of the remaining black strip to make strip set C. Press the seam allowances toward the black strips. Crosscut the strip sets into the number of 1½"-wide segments indicated.

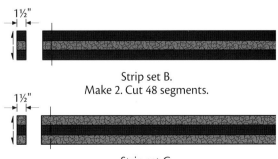

1½"

Strip set B.
Make 2. Cut 48 segments.

1½"

Strip set C.
Make 1. Cut 24 segments.

3. Sew a B segment to each side of a C segment to make a Nine Patch block. Press the seam allowances toward the B segments. Repeat to make a total of 24 blocks.

Make 24.

4. To make a half-nine-patch unit, place your rotary ruler on one of the Nine Patch blocks with the ¼" line aligned with the points of diagonal corners as shown. Cut across the block. Discard the upper piece. Repeat to make a total of 12 units.

¼" line

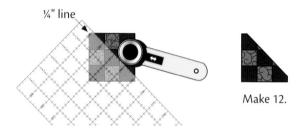

Make 12.

Assembling the Quilt Top

1. Refer to the quilt assembly diagram to lay out the floral 9½" squares, the floral setting triangles, the floral corner triangles, and the sashing blocks and units into diagonal rows as shown. Sew the pieces in each row together. Press the seam allowances toward the Elongated Rail Fence blocks. Sew the rows together. Press the seam allowances toward the block rows.

2. Join two red 1"-wide strips together end to end to make one long strip. Repeat to make a total of four pieced strips. Join two black 4½"-wide strips together end to end to make one long strip. Repeat to make a total of four pieced strips.

3. Refer to "Borders" on page 12 to apply the red inner border, and then the black outer border using either the butted- or mitered-corners technique.

Quilt assembly

Quilting and Binding

1. Refer to "Preparing the Quilt Sandwich" on page 13 to layer the quilt top, batting, and backing.
2. Hand or machine quilt as desired.
3. Refer to "Binding" on page 14 to bind the quilt edges with the red 2"-wide strips.

Quilting Suggestion

A very simple yet effective way of quilting this quilt is to stitch in the ditch of the narrow inner border and each of the sashing elements. For the outer border, I quilted three roses in one corner and circled the quilt with a feather motif. The minimal quilting really allows the beauty of the large-scale print to shine through, yet is sufficient to hold the layers together for years and years to come.

Sherbet Stars

Pieced and quilted by Karen Sievert

I just love this quilt. There's some-thing so soft, sweet, and inviting about it. With just one block stitched in four colorways of the same fabric line to achieve a blended look, this quilt couldn't be easier to make. Carrying each of the colors into the borders adds to the quilt's visual appeal, while using a high-loft batting makes it extra snuggly.

Finished quilt: 79" x 91½"
Finished block: 12½" x 12½"

Materials

Yardages are based on 42"-wide fabric unless otherwise indicated. This quilt is made from four colorways—pink, purple, yellow, and green—from the same fabric line to achieve a blended look.

1 yard *each* of pink, purple, yellow, and green large-scale floral print for blocks

1 yard *each* of medium-value pink, purple, yellow, and green tone-on-tone print for blocks and outer border

¾ yard *each* of light-value pink, purple, yellow and green tone-on-tone print for blocks and inner border

⅓ yard *each* of pink, purple, yellow, and green plaid for blocks

¼ yard *each* of pink, purple, yellow, and green small-scale floral print for blocks

⅝ yard of light-value fabric for binding

2½ yards of 108"-wide fabric for backing

87" x 100" piece of batting (high-loft batting was used on the quilt shown)

Cutting

All measurements include ¼"-wide seam allowances.

From *each* of the light-value tone-on-tone prints, cut:

3 strips, 3½" x 42"; crosscut into 32 squares, 3½" x 3½" (128 total)

1 strip, 4¼" x 42"; crosscut into 8 squares, 4¼" x 4¼". Cut each square into quarters diagonally to yield 32 triangles (128 total).

3 strips, 2½" x 42" (12 total)

From *each* of the small-scale floral prints, cut:

1 strip, 4¼" x 42"; crosscut into 8 squares, 4¼" x 4¼". Cut each square into quarters diagonally to yield 32 triangles (128 total).

From *each* of the plaid fabrics, cut:

1 strip, 3½" x 42"; crosscut into 4 squares, 3½" x 3½" (16 total)

1 strip, 4¼" x 42"; crosscut into 8 squares, 4¼" x 4¼". Cut each square into quarters diagonally to yield 32 triangles (128 total).

From *each* of the medium tone-on-tone prints, cut:

1 strip, 3½" x 42"; crosscut into 4 squares, 3½" x 3½" (16 total)

1 strip, 4¼" x 42"; crosscut into 8 squares, 4¼" x 4¼". Cut each square into quarters diagonally to yield 32 triangles (128 total).

3 strips, 6½" x 42" (12 total)

From *each* of the large-scale floral prints, cut:

3 strips, 7⅛" x 42"; crosscut into 16 squares, 7⅛" x 7⅛". Cut each square in half diagonally to yield 32 triangles (128 total).

From the light-value fabric for binding, cut:

9 strips, 2" x 42"

Piecing the Blocks

1. Lay out one light pink tone-on-tone triangle, one small-scale floral triangle, and two pink plaid triangles as shown. Sew the triangles into pairs. Press the seam allowances toward the pink plaid triangles. Sew the pairs together to make an hourglass unit. Press the seam allowance in either direction. Repeat to make a total of 16 units. Trim the dog-ears.

Make 16.

2. Lay out four units from step 1, four light pink tone-on-tone 3½" squares, and one medium pink 3½" tone-on-tone square into three horizontal rows. Sew the pieces in each row together, pressing the seam allowances as indicated. Sew the rows together. Press the seam allowances toward the top and bottom rows. Repeat to make a total of four star units.

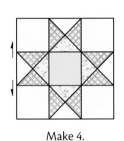

Make 4.

3. Repeat step 1 to make 16 hourglass units, substituting two medium pink tone-on-tone triangles for the plaid triangles.

Make 16.

4. Lay out four units from step 2, four light pink 3½" squares, and one pink plaid 3½" square into three horizontal rows. Repeat step 2 to sew the pieces together to make four additional star units.

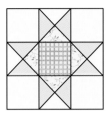

Make 4.

5. Sew one of each of the four colors of the large-scale floral triangles to the corners of the star units, adding opposite sides first and making sure to always place the same color in the same corner. Press the seam allowances toward the large-scale floral triangles. Trim the dog-ears.

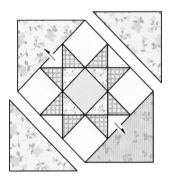

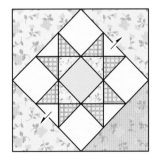

Make 4.

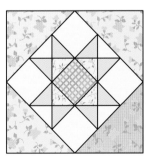

Make 4.

6. Repeat steps 1–5 to make eight blocks *each* of the remaining three colorways for a total of 32 blocks.

Assembling the Quilt Top

1. Refer to the quilt assembly diagram to lay out the blocks in six rows of five blocks each, alternating colors in a manner that is pleasing to you and always making sure that the top-left triangle is purple. You will have two blocks left over. I used mine to make a coordinating throw pillow, but you could also use them for your quilt label. Sew the blocks in each row together. Press the seam allowances in opposite directions from row to row. Sew the rows together. Press the seam allowances in one direction.

2. Sew the three light pink tone-on-tone 2½" x 42" strips together end to end, making one long strip. Repeat with each of the three remaining colorways to make a total of four pieced inner-border strips. Repeat with the medium-value tone-on-tone 6½" x 42" strips to make a total of four pieced outer-border strips.

3. With right sides together, sew the light pink border strip to the medium pink border strip along one long edge. Repeat for the remaining three colorways.

4. Referring to "Borders" on pages 12, sew the borders to the quilt top, positioning the light-value strips closest to the quilt center and using the mitered-corners technique.

Quilting and Binding

1. Refer to "Preparing the Quilt Sandwich" on page 13 to layer the quilt top, batting, and backing.
2. Hand or machine quilt as desired.
3. Refer to "Binding" on page 14 to bind the quilt edges with the light-value 2"-wide strips.

Quilting Suggestion

To achieve the soft look of the quilt shown, use a high-loft batting because it really makes the quilting pop. I outline quilted the star portion of the blocks and stitched a fleur-de-lis motif in the areas where the four large-scale floral triangles come together. In the outer border, I used a pastel variegated thread to quilt a freehand feather, which draws the eye to the uniqueness of the four-colored border as it circles the quilt.

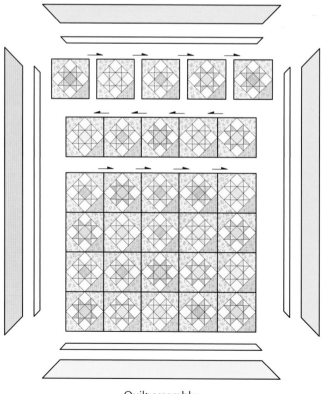

Quilt assembly

Contrasting Stars

Pieced by Karen Sievert. Quilted by Monica Forsyth.

One of the things I've always loved about quilting is that we can all make the same quilt but each one can look entirely different based on our color and fabric choices. I've seen it happen time and time again, and it's certainly the case here. The block in this quilt is the same as in "Sherbet Stars" on page 23 and is a great example of how one block can have several different looks. Placing a light-colored flange strip through the center of the inner-border blocks gives the illusion that the blocks are on point, plus the contrast adds an element of surprise, giving the quilt a charm and grace all its own.

Finished quilt: 87½" x 100"
Finished Star block: 12½" x 12½"
Finished inner-border block: 12½" x 6¼"
  and 6¼" x 6¼"

Materials

Yardages are based on 42"-wide fabric unless otherwise indicated.

4⅓ yards of large-scale dark floral for pieced inner border, outer border, and binding
2⅓ yards of medium-scale dark floral for blocks and pieced inner border
2 yards of dark paisley print for blocks and pieced inner border
1¾ yards of light neutral background fabric for blocks
1¼ yards of small-scale light floral for blocks and pieced inner-border flange
⅝ yard of burgundy fabric for blocks
⅝ yard of green fabric for blocks
2¾ yards of 108"-wide fabric for backing
95" x 108" piece of batting

Cutting

All measurements include ¼-wide seam allowances.

From the burgundy fabric, cut:
4 strips, 4¼" x 42"; crosscut into 30 squares, 4¼" x 4¼". Cut each square into quarters diagonally to yield 120 triangles.

From the small-scale light floral, cut:
4 strips, 4¼" x 42"; crosscut into 30 squares, 4¼" x 4¼". Cut each square into quarters diagonally to yield 120 triangles.
12 strips, 1½" x 42"; crosscut into 48 rectangles, 1½" x 10"

From the light neutral background fabric, cut:
11 strips, 3½" x 42"; crosscut into 120 squares, 3½" x 3½"
4 strips, 4¼" x 42"; crosscut into 30 squares, 4¼" x 4¼". Cut each square into quarters diagonally to yield 120 triangles.

From the medium-scale dark floral, cut:
3 strips, 3½" x 42"; crosscut into 30 squares, 3½" x 3½"
9 strips, 7⅛" x 42"; crosscut into 42 squares, 7⅛" x 7⅛". Cut each square in half diagonally to yield 84 triangles.

From the green fabric, cut:
4 strips, 4¼" x 42"; crosscut into 30 squares, 4¼" x 4¼". Cut each square into quarters diagonally to yield 120 triangles.

From the dark paisley print, cut:
9 strips, 7⅛" x 42"; crosscut into 42 squares, 7⅛" x 7⅛". Cut each square in half diagonally to yield 84 triangles.

From the large-scale dark floral, cut:
3 strips, 13¾" x 42"; crosscut into 6 squares, 13¾" x 13¾". Cut each square into quarters diagonally to yield 24 triangles (2 triangles left over).
2 squares, 7⅛" x 7⅛"; cut each square in half diagonally to yield 4 triangles
11 strips, 6½" x 42"
10 strips, 2" x 42"

Piecing the Star Blocks

1. Lay out two burgundy triangles, one small-scale floral triangle, and one background triangle as shown. Sew the triangles into pairs. Press the seam allowances toward the burgundy triangles. Sew the pairs together to make an hourglass unit. Press the seam allowances in either direction. Repeat to make a total of 60 units. Trim the dog-ears.

Make 60.

2. Lay out four units from step 1, four background 3½" squares, and one medium-scale floral 3½" square into three horizontal rows. Sew the pieces in each row together, pressing the seam allowances as indicated. Sew the rows together. Press the seam allowances toward the top and bottom rows. Repeat to make a total of 15 burgundy star units.

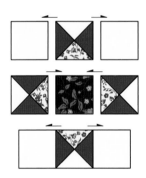 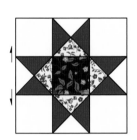

Make 15.

3. Repeat steps 1 and 2, substituting the green triangles for the burgundy triangles, to make 15 green star units.

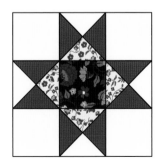

Make 15.

4. Sew medium-scale floral triangles to opposite sides of each burgundy and each green star unit. Press the seam allowances toward the triangles. Sew paisley triangles to the remaining two sides of each unit. Press the seam allowances toward the triangles. Trim the dog-ears.

Make 15.   Make 15.

Assembling the Quilt Top

1. Refer to the quilt assembly diagram to lay out the blocks into six rows of five blocks each, alternating the red and green Star blocks in each row and from row to row. Sew the blocks in each row together. Press the seam allowances in opposite directions from row to row. Sew the rows together. Press the seam allowances in one direction.

2. Press each small-scale floral 1½" x 10" rectangle in half lengthwise, wrong sides together, to make a flat flange.

3. Pin a flange strip along both short edges of 22 large-scale floral print triangles cut from the 13¾" squares, aligning the raw edges of the flanges with the raw edges of the triangles. The flanges will be longer than the short edges of the triangle; you will trim off the excess after sewing. Discard the remaining two triangles or save them for another project.

4. On 10 of the pinned large-scale floral triangles, sew a medium-scale dark floral triangle to the left edge, and then sew a paisley triangle to the right edge. Press the seam allowances toward the paisley and medium-scale floral triangles. Do not press the flange; it should continue to have the folded edges pointing in toward the large-scale floral. Trim the dog-ears and excess flange even with the edges of the blocks.

Make 10.

5. Sew five blocks together side by side to make a border strip. Repeat to make a total of two strips. Refer to the quilt assembly diagram to sew these borders to the top and bottom edges of the quilt top, making sure the large-scale floral triangles are pointing toward the center of the quilt.

6. On each of the 12 remaining pinned large-scale floral triangles, sew a paisley triangle to the left edge, and then sew a medium-scale dark floral triangle to the right edge. Press the seam allowances toward the medium-scale floral and paisley triangles. Again, do not press the flange out. Trim the dog-ears and excess flange.

Make 12.

7. On each of the four large-scale floral triangles cut from the 7⅛" squares, pin a piece of flange along the long edge of the triangles, aligning the raw edges.

Make 4.

8. Position a paisley print triangle over two pinned triangles and a medium-scale floral triangle over the remaining two pinned triangles. Sew the triangles together along the long edges. Press the seam allowances toward the paisley and medium-scale floral triangles. Trim the dog-ears and excess flange.

Make 2.   Make 2.

9. Refer to the quilt assembly diagram on page 31 to sew together six blocks from step 6 and two blocks from step 8 for the left border. Press the seam allowances in the opposite direction as the quilt-top rows. Sew the border to the left side of the quilt top. Repeat with the remaining blocks for the right border and sew it to the quilt top.

10. Referring to "Borders" on pages 12, sew the large-scale floral 6½"-wide outer borders to the quilt top using the butted-corners technique.

Quilting and Binding

1. Refer to "Preparing the Quilt Sandwich" on page 13 to layer the quilt top, batting, and backing.
2. Hand or machine quilt as desired.
3. Refer to "Binding" on page 14 to bind the quilt edges with the large-scale floral 2"-wide strips.

Quilting Suggestion

Monica did a wonderful job of quilting this quilt. All the star elements were outline quilted and the pieced border was outline and echo quilted. A wrought-iron motif was stitched into the areas where the four corner triangles meet and a matching pattern was quilted into the border. This quilt is a keeper and a joy to have in any home!

Quilt assembly

Roman Tile

Pieced and quilted by Karen Sievert

Because my husband is in the military, we had the opportunity to live in Italy for about two years. Every time I see this quilt it takes me back there. It is so reminiscent of the beautiful tile work we saw in homes and piazzas across the country. While it may look complicated, this quilt is really quite simple to put together. And the two-color border really sets off the blocks.

Finished quilt: 71½" x 86¼"
Finished block: 10½" x 10½"

Materials

Yardages are based on 42"-wide fabric unless otherwise indicated.

3¼ yards of white fabric for blocks, setting triangles, border, and binding
3 yards of black fabric for blocks, setting triangles, border, and binding
1½ yards of Asian print for blocks
⅞ yard of dark green tone-on-tone print for block A
⅞ yard of small-scale print for blocks
⅝ yard of medium green print for blocks
2¼ yards of 108"-wide fabric for backing
80" x 95" piece of batting

Cutting

All measurements include ¼"-wide seam allowances.

From the medium green print, cut:
9 strips, 2" x 42"

From the small-scale print, cut:
13 strips, 2" x 42"

From the white fabric, cut:
9 strips, 2" x 42"; crosscut 4 strips into 80 squares, 2" x 2"
16 strips, 2⅜" x 42"; crosscut into 256 squares, 2⅜" x 2⅜"
2 squares, 16" x 16"; cut each square into quarters diagonally to yield 8 triangles (1 left over)
1 square, 8⅜" x 8⅜"; cut in half diagonally to yield 2 triangles (1 left over)
1 square, 8⅝" x 8⅝"; cut into quarters diagonally to yield 4 triangles (2 left over)
5 strips, 6½" x 42"

From the dark green tone-on-tone print, cut:
1 strip, 2" x 42"; crosscut into 20 squares, 2" x 2"
10 strips, 2⅜" x 42"; crosscut into 160 squares, 2⅜" x 2⅜"

From the Asian print, cut:
6 strips, 2⅜" x 42"; crosscut into 96 squares, 2⅜" x 2⅜"
16 strips, 2" x 42"; crosscut 14 strips into:
    80 rectangles, 2" x 5"
    72 squares, 2" x 2"

From the black fabric, cut:
16 strips, 2" x 42"; crosscut 6 strips into:
    48 squares, 2" x 2"
    24 rectangles, 2" x 5"
2 strips, 5" x 42"
5 strips, 6½" x 42"
2 squares, 16" x 16"; cut each square into quarters diagonally to yield 8 triangles (1 left over)
1 square, 8⅜" x 8⅜"; cut in half diagonally to yield 2 triangles (1 left over)
1 square, 8⅝" x 8⅝"; cut into quarters diagonally to yield 4 triangles (2 left over)

Piecing Block A

1. With right sides together, sew a medium green strip to a small-scale print strip along one long edge to make a strip set. Repeat to make a total of nine strip sets. Press the seam allowances toward the medium green strips. Crosscut the strip sets into 160 segments, 2" wide.

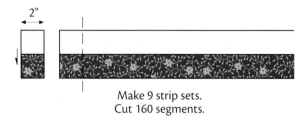

Make 9 strip sets.
Cut 160 segments.

2. Sew two segments together to make a four-patch unit. Repeat to make a total of 80 units.

Make 80.

3. Draw a diagonal line from corner to corner on the wrong sides of 160 white 2⅜" squares. With the marked squares on top, layer each square with a dark green 2⅜" square, right sides together. Stitch ¼" away from both sides of the drawn line. Cut the squares apart on the line to yield 320 half-square-triangle units. Press the seam allowances toward the dark green fabric. Trim the dog-ears.

Make 320.

4. Sew two half-square-triangle units together, positioning the green triangle on the bottom left. Press the seam allowance toward the left-hand unit. Repeat to make a total of 80 units.

Make 80.

5. Sew a unit from step 4 to the right edge of each four-patch unit from step 2, making sure the green squares are positioned in the upper-right and lower-left corners. Press the seam allowances toward the four-patch units.

Make 80.

6. Sew two half-square-triangle units and one white 2" square together as shown. Press the seam allowances toward the center half-square-triangle unit. Repeat to make a total of 80 units.

Make 80.

7. Join the units from step 6 to the top of each unit from step 5. Press the seam allowances toward the four-patch units.

Make 80.

8. Lay out four units from step 7, four Asian print 2" x 5" rectangles, and one dark green square into three horizontal rows. Sew the pieces in each row together. Press the seam allowances toward the Asian print rectangles. Sew the rows together. Press the seam allowances toward the center row. Repeat to make a total of 20 blocks.

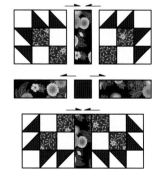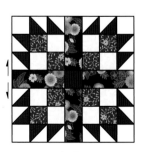

Block A.
Make 20.

Piecing Block B

1. Draw a diagonal line from corner to corner on the wrong side of each of the remaining 96 white 2⅜" squares. With the marked squares on top, layer each square with an Asian print 2⅜" square, right sides together. Stitch ¼" away from both sides of the drawn line. Cut the squares apart on the line to yield 192 half-square-triangle units. Press the seam allowances toward the Asian print. Trim the dog-ears.

Make 192.

2. Sew a half-square-triangle unit to each side of an Asian print 2" square. Press the seam allowances toward the square. Repeat to make a total of 72 units.

Make 72.

3. Sew a unit from step 2 to each side of a black 2" x 5" rectangle. Press the seam allowances toward the rectangle. Repeat to make a total of 24 units.

Make 24.

4. Join black squares to the ends of each of the remaining units from step 2, and then sew a half-square-triangle unit from step 1 to the ends of those units. Press the seam allowances toward the black squares.

Make 24.

5. Sew Asian print 2" x 42" strips to both long edges of a black 2" x 42" strip to make strip set A. Press the

seam allowances toward the black strip. Crosscut the strip set into 12 segments, 2" wide.

2"

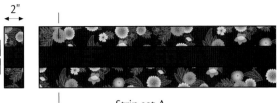

Strip set A.
Make 1. Cut 12 segments.

6. Sew two black 2" x 42" strips, two small-scale print 2" x 42" strips, and one black 5" x 42" strip together along the long edges to make strip set B. Press the seam allowances toward the black strips. Repeat to make a total of two strip sets. Crosscut the strip sets into 24 segments, 2" wide.

2"

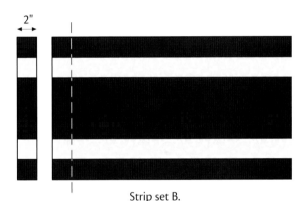

Strip set B.
Make 2. Cut 24 segments.

7. Lay out two units from step 3, two units from step 4, one strip-set A segment, and two strip-set B segments into five horizontal rows. Sew the pieces in each row together. Press the seam allowances of the third row toward the strip-set A segment. Sew the rows together. Press the seam allowances toward the strip-set B segments. Repeat to make a total of 12 blocks.

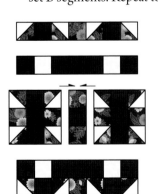

Block B.
Make 12.

Assembling the Quilt Top

1. Sew one black and one white 8⅝" triangle together along the short edges to make a pieced setting triangle for the bottom-left corner. Repeat to make one additional pieced setting triangle as shown for the top-right corner.

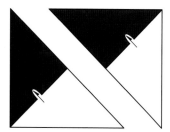

Make 1 of each.

2. Refer to the quilt assembly diagram to lay out the blocks and setting triangles into diagonal rows. Sew the pieces in each row together. Press the seam allowances in opposite directions from row to row. Sew the rows together. Press the seam allowances away from the center row.

3. Using the white and black 6½"-wide strips and referring to "Borders" on page 12, apply the border to the quilt top using the mitered-corners technique.

Quilt assembly

Quilting and Binding

1. Refer to "Preparing the Quilt Sandwich" on page 13 to layer the quilt top, batting, and backing.

2. Hand or machine quilt as desired.

3. Sew the black 2" x 42" strips together end to end to make one long strip. Repeat with the white 2" x 42" strips. Press each of the pieced strips in half lengthwise, wrong sides together.

4. Beginning at the bottom-left corner and leaving a 2" tail, apply the black binding as described in "Binding" on page 14. Stop ¼" away from the top-right corner; backstitch to secure. Clip off the excess black fabric, leaving a 2" tail.

2" tail

2" tail

5. Beginning at the top-right corner and leaving a 2" tail, apply the white binding as described in "Binding." Stop ¼" away from the bottom-left corner; backstitch to secure. Clip off the excess white fabric, leaving a 2" tail.

6. Fold the quilt in half at a 45° angle, right sides together, so that the two binding tails at the bottom-left corner are on top of each other and the two binding tails at the top-right corner are on top of each other.

7. On each of the unstitched binding corners, mark a dot on the binding where the stitching ended (¼" start and stop point) and another straight up from this dot at the fold on the top binding strip. Draw a 90° angle that points out, equidistant from each dot. Stitch on this line, and then trim ¼" away from the stitching line.

8. Refer to "Binding" to fold the binding to the back and hand stitch it in place.

Fold of quilt

Quilting Suggestion

This patchwork really benefits from outline quilting. I outline quilted the white and Asian pieces and crosshatched the four-patch units. The border and setting triangles give the quilter an incredible space for creative freedom in quilting. I quilted a freehand feather that curls from the border into the setting triangle and seamlessly transitions from black to white! Motifs in the setting triangles with a matching border pattern would also be very effective and visually stunning.

Star Flower

Designed and quilted by Karen Sievert. Pieced by Martha Williams.

This quilt was so much fun to design. I really liked both blocks, but found, much to my delight, that when joined, the lines between them blurred. It's very difficult to pick out where one block starts and the other ends—which is why they're better together.

Finished quilt: 80½" x 104½"
Finished block: 12" x 12"

Materials

Yardages are based on 42"-wide fabric unless otherwise indicated.

3⅞ yards of beige fabric for blocks and inner border
3½ yards of floral for blocks and outer border
1⅞ yards of navy fabric for blocks
1⅜ yards of light blue fabric for block B, flat flange, and binding
⅞ yard of purple fabric for block B
3⅛ yards of 90"-wide fabric for backing
88" x 112" piece of batting

Cutting

All measurements include ¼"-wide seam allowances.

From the navy fabric, cut:
4 strips, 3⅞" x 42"; crosscut into 34 squares, 3⅞" x 3⅞". Cut each square in half diagonally to yield 68 triangles.
10 strips, 4¼" x 42"; crosscut into 88 squares, 4¼" x 4¼". Cut each square into quarters diagonally to yield 352 triangles.

From the floral, cut:
3 strips, 4¾" x 42"; crosscut into 17 squares, 4¾" x 4¾"
5 strips, 2⅝" x 42"; crosscut into 68 squares, 2⅝" x 2⅝"
13 strips, 6½" x 42"; crosscut 3 strips into 18 squares, 6½" x 6½"

From the beige fabric, cut:
7 strips, 3½" x 42"; crosscut into 68 squares, 3½" x 3½"
12 strips, 4¼" x 42"; crosscut into 104 squares, 4¼" x 4¼". Cut each square into quarters diagonally to yield 416 triangles.
4 strips, 3⅞" x 42"; crosscut into 36 squares, 3⅞" x 3⅞"
8 strips, 4½" x 42"

From the light blue fabric, cut:
4 strips, 3⅞" x 42"; crosscut into 36 squares, 3⅞" x 3⅞"
8 strips, 1" x 42"
10 strips, 2" x 42"

From the purple fabric, cut:
6 strips, 4¼" x 42"; crosscut into 54 squares, 4¼" x 4¼". Cut each square into quarters diagonally to yield 216 triangles.

Piecing Block A

1. Sew navy 3⅞" triangles to opposite sides of a floral 4¾" square. Press the seam allowances toward the navy triangles. Repeat for the remaining two sides of the square. Repeat to make a total of 17 units. Trim the dog-ears.

Make 17.

2. Sew beige triangles to opposite sides of a floral 2⅝" square. Press the seam allowances toward the beige triangles. Repeat to make a total of 68 units. Trim the dog-ears.

Make 68.

3. Sew a navy 4¼" triangle to a beige triangle. Press the seam allowances toward the beige triangle. Repeat to make a total of 136 pieced triangles.

Make 136.

4. Sew a pieced triangle to the long edges of each unit from step 2. Press the seam allowances toward the pieced triangles.

Make 68.

5. Lay out one unit from step 1, four units from step 4, and four beige 3½" squares into three horizontal rows. Sew the pieces in each row together. Press the seam allowances in the directions indicated. Sew the

rows together. Press the seam allowances toward the middle row. Repeat to make a total of 17 blocks.

Block A.
Make 17.

Piecing Block B

1. Draw a diagonal line from corner to corner on the wrong sides of each beige 3⅞" square. With the marked squares on top, layer each square with a light blue 3⅞" square, right sides together. Stitch ¼" away from both sides of the drawn line. Cut the squares apart on the line to yield 72 half-square-triangle units. Press the seam allowances toward the beige triangles. Trim the dog-ears.

Make 72.

2. Sew a purple triangle to a navy 4¼" triangle along the long edges. Press the seam allowance toward the navy triangle. Repeat to make a total of 72 pieced squares. Trim the dog-ears.

Make 72.

3. Sew beige triangles to the navy edges of each unit from step 2. Press the seam allowances toward the beige triangles. Trim the dog-ears.

Make 72.

4. Sew the remaining purple and navy triangles together along the short edges to make 72 of each of the pieced triangles shown. Press the seam allowances toward the navy triangles.

Make 72.

Make 72.

5. Sew one of each of the pieced triangles made in step 4 to each of the units made in step 3. Press the seam allowances toward the pieced triangles.

Make 72.

6. Lay out one floral 6½" square, four half-square-triangle units made in step 1, and four units made in step 5 into three horizontal rows. Sew the pieces in each row together. Press the seam allowances in the

directions indicated. Sew the rows together. Repeat to make a total of 18 blocks.

Block B.
Make 18.

Assembling the Quilt Top

1. Refer to the quilt assembly diagram on page 42 to lay out the blocks in seven rows of five blocks each, alternating the blocks in each row and from row to row. Rotate the blocks as needed so the seam allowances oppose each other. Sew the blocks in each row together. Press the seam allowances in opposite directions from row to row. Sew the rows together. Press the seam allowances in one direction.
2. Using the beige 4½"-wide strips and referring to "Borders" on page 12, apply the inner border to the quilt top using the butted-corners technique.
3. Sew the light blue 1"-wide strips together end to end to make one long strip of flat flange. Press the strip in half lengthwise, wrong sides together. Measure the length of the quilt top through the center and cut two pieces from the flange strip that are the exact length measured. With the raw edges aligned, sew the flange strips to the sides of the quilt top using a *scant* ¼"-wide seam allowance.

4. Measure the width of the quilt top through the center and cut two pieces from the remainder of the flange strips that are the exact length measured. Sew these strips to the top and bottom edges of the quilt top in the same manner as for the side flange strips.
5. Using the floral 6½"-wide strips and referring to "Borders," apply the outer border to the quilt top using the butted-corners technique.

Quilting and Binding

1. Refer to "Preparing the Quilt Sandwich" on page 13 to layer the quilt top, batting, and backing.
2. Hand or machine quilt as desired.
3. Refer to "Binding" on page 14 to bind the quilt edges with the light blue 2"-wide strips.

Quilting Suggestion

I had a lot of fun quilting this quilt. I outline quilted most of the patchwork and stitched freehand feathers in the large beige spaces and inner border and a floral meandering design in the outer border.

Quilt assembly

Pieced and quilted by Karen Sievert

This two-block combo is a winner and another great example of how two blocks, individually beautiful, can become magic together. The soft, subtle pinks, yellows, and greens give this quilt a sweet simplicity that reminds me of my childhood. This quilt is one that any little girl would love to have, and maybe some big girls too!

Finished quilt: 58½" x 88½"
Finished block: 15" x 15"

Materials

Yardages are based on 42"-wide fabric unless otherwise indicated.

2⅜ yards of large-scale floral for blocks, outer border, and binding

1⅜ yards of light pink fabric for block B and inner border

1⅛ yards of medium green fabric for blocks

⅞ yards of light yellow fabric for blocks

⅞ yard of light green print for block A

⅔ yard of medium yellow print for blocks

½ yard of small-scale pink floral for block A

½ yard of medium-scale pink floral for block A

⅜ yard of small-scale yellow floral for block B

⅞ yards of 108"-wide fabric for backing

66" x 96" piece of batting (high-loft batting used on quilt shown)

Cutting

All measurements include ¼-wide seam allowances.

From the medium yellow print, cut:
3 strips, 3" x 42"
3 strips, 3⅜" x 42"; crosscut into 28 squares, 3⅜" x 3⅜"

From the light green print, cut:
3 strips, 3" x 42"
3 strips, 5½" x 42"; crosscut into 32 rectangles, 3" x 5½"

From the light yellow fabric, cut:
3 strips, 6¼" x 42"; crosscut into 15 squares, 6¼" x 6¼". Cut each square into quarters diagonally to yield 60 triangles.
2 strips, 3⅜" x 42"; crosscut into 14 squares, 3⅜" x 3⅜"

From the medium green fabric, cut:
2 strips, 6¼" x 42"; crosscut into 8 squares, 6¼" x 6¼". Cut each square into quarters diagonally to yield 32 triangles.
6 strips, 3⅜" x 42"; crosscut into 56 squares, 3⅜" x 3⅜". Cut 28 squares in half diagonally to yield 56 triangles.

From the small-scale pink floral, cut:
2 strips, 6¼" x 42"; crosscut into 8 squares, 6¼" x 6¼". Cut each square into quarters diagonally to yield 32 triangles.

From the medium-scale pink floral, cut:
2 strips, 6¼" x 42"; crosscut into 8 squares, 6¼" x 6¼". Cut each square into quarters diagonally to yield 32 triangles.

From the large-scale floral, cut:
11 strips, 5½" x 42"; crosscut 3 strips into 15 squares, 5½" x 5½"
8 strips, 2" x 42"

From the small-scale yellow floral, cut:
3 strips, 3⅜" x 42"; crosscut into 28 squares, 3⅜" x 3⅜". Cut each square in half diagonally to yield 56 triangles.

From the light pink fabric, cut:
2 strips, 6¼" x 42"; crosscut into 7 squares, 6¼" x 6¼". Cut each square into quarters diagonally to yield 28 triangles.
3 strips, 3" x 42"; crosscut into 28 squares, 3" x 3"
2 strips, 3⅜" x 42"; crosscut into 14 squares, 3⅜" x 3⅜"
7 strips, 2" x 42"

Piecing Block A

1. With right sides together, sew a medium yellow 3" x 42" strip to a light green 3" x 42" strip along one long edge to make a strip set. Repeat to make a total of three strip sets. Press the seam allowances toward the green strips. Crosscut the strip sets into 32 segments, 3" wide.

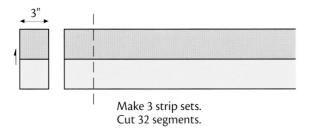

Make 3 strip sets.
Cut 32 segments.

2. Sew 16 of the light green rectangles to the left edge of 16 segments from step 1. Sew the remaining light green rectangles to the right edge of the remaining segments from step 1. Press the seam allowances toward the rectangles.

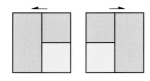

Make 16 of each.

3. Lay out one light yellow, one medium green, and two small-scale pink floral 6¼" triangles as shown. Sew the triangles into pairs. Press the seam allowances toward the pink triangles. Sew the pairs together to make pieced squares. Press the seam allowance in either direction. Repeat to make a total of 16 pieced squares. Repeat to make another 16 pieced squares, substituting the medium-scale pink floral triangles for the small-scale floral triangles. Trim the dog-ears.

Make 16 of each.

4. Lay out one large-scale floral 5½" square, two of each of the units from step 2, and four matching units from step 3 into three horizontal rows. Sew the pieces in each row together. Press the seam allowances in the directions indicated. Sew the rows together. Press the seam allowances toward the center row. Repeat to make a total of eight blocks.

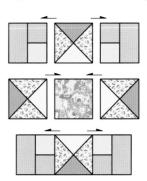

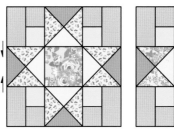

Block A.
Make 4 of each.

Piecing Block B

1. Draw a line from corner to corner on the wrong sides of each light yellow and each medium yellow 3⅜" square. With the marked squares on top, layer each light yellow square with a light pink 3⅜" square and each medium yellow square with a medium green 3⅜" square. Stitch ¼" away from both sides of the drawn lines. Cut the squares apart on the lines to yield 28 light yellow/light pink half-square-triangle units and 56 medium yellow/medium green half-square-triangle units. Press the seam allowances toward the light pink and medium green triangles. Trim the dog-ears.

Make 28.   Make 56.

2. Sew a small-scale yellow floral triangle to one short side of a light yellow triangle. Press the seam allowance toward the floral print triangle. Repeat on the opposite side. Repeat to make a total of 28 light yellow flying-geese units. Trim the dog-ears. Repeat with the light pink triangles and medium green triangles to make a total of 28 light pink flying-geese units.

Make 28.   Make 28.

3. Sew each light yellow flying-geese unit to a light pink flying-geese unit along the long edges. Press the seam allowances toward the light pink units.

Make 28.

4. Sew a light pink 3" square to a medium yellow/medium green half-square-triangle unit from step 1. Press the seam allowance toward the pink square. Repeat to make a total of 28 units.

Make 28.

5. Sew a light yellow/light pink half-square-triangle unit to each of the remaining medium yellow/medium green half-square-triangle units. Press the seam allowances toward the yellow/pink units.

Make 28.

6. Sew a unit from step 4 to each unit from step 5. Press the seam allowances toward the units with the yellow/pink square.

Make 28.

7. Lay out one large-scale floral 5½" square, four of the units from step 3, and four of the units from step 6 into three horizontal rows. Sew the pieces in each row together. Press the seam allowances in the directions indicated. Sew the rows together. Press the seam allowances toward the top and bottom rows. Repeat to make a total of seven blocks.

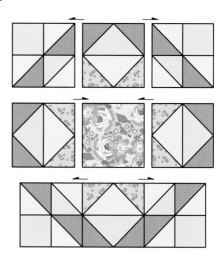

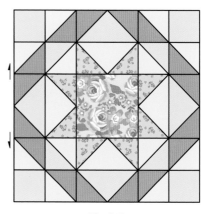

Block B.
Make 7.

Assembling the Quilt Top

1. Refer to the quilt assembly diagram to lay out the blocks in five rows of three blocks each, alternating the blocks in each row and from row to row. Rotate the blocks as needed so the seam allowances oppose each other. Sew the blocks in each row together. Press the seam allowances in opposite directions from row to row. Sew the rows together. Press the seam allowances in one direction.
2. Using the seven light pink 2"-wide strips and referring to "Borders" on page 12, apply the inner border to the quilt top using the butted-corners technique. Repeat for the outer border, using the remaining eight large-scale floral 5½"-wide strips.

Quilt assembly

Quilting and Binding

1. Refer to "Preparing the Quilt Sandwich" on page 13 to layer the quilt top, batting, and backing.
2. Hand or machine quilt as desired.
3. Refer to "Binding" on page 14 to bind the quilt edges with the large-scale floral 2"-wide strips.

Quilting Suggestion

This quilt gets a little added pop by using a high-loft batting. I simply outline quilted the majority of the patchwork, put feather motifs in one of the block frames, and channel quilted the other block frames. The feather in the border complements the featherwork in the frame. However you decide to quilt it, this quilt is sure to make you smile.

Sew Dear

Designed and quilted by Karen Sievert. Pieced by Martha Williams.

I had this wonderful fabric with motifs of quilting ladies, quilting slogans, and quilting tools. Because it was a large-scale print, I just kept holding on to it, not wanting to cut it apart. This pattern really lends itself for use with large-scale prints, and especially for large-scale themed prints. I call this "Sew Dear" because I think it would make a great gift for any one of my sewing buddies!

Finished quilt: 47½" x 59½"
Finished block: 12" x 12"

Materials

Yardages are based on 42"-wide fabric unless otherwise indicated.

1⅞ yards of star print for blocks and outer border
1¼ yards of pink fabric for blocks
1 yard of black fabric for block A, inner border, and
    binding
⅔ yard of large-scale print for blocks
1⅝ yards of 90"-wide fabric for backing
55" x 67" piece of batting

Cutting

All measurements include ¼"-wide seam allowances.

From the pink fabric, cut:
2 strips, 9¼" x 42"; crosscut into 6 squares, 9¼" x 9¼".
    Cut each square into quarters diagonally to yield
    24 triangles.
2 strips, 4⅛" x 42"; crosscut into 12 squares, 4⅛" x 4⅛".
    Cut each square into quarters diagonally to yield
    48 triangles.
2 strips, 5¼" x 42"; crosscut into 12 squares, 5¼" x 5¼".
    Cut each square into quarters diagonally to yield
    48 triangles.

From the black fabric, cut:
2 strips, 4⅛" x 42"; crosscut into 12 squares, 4⅛" x 4⅛".
    Cut each square into quarters diagonally to yield
    48 triangles.
5 strips, 1" x 42"
6 strips, 2" x 42"

From the star print, cut:
1 strip, 2⅞" x 42"; crosscut into 12 squares, 2⅞" x 2⅞".
    Cut each square in half diagonally to yield 24 triangles.
3 strips, 3⅜" x 42"; crosscut into 24 squares, 3⅜" x 3⅜"
2 strips, 4⅞" x 42"; crosscut into 12 squares, 4⅞" x 4⅞".
    Cut each square in half diagonally to yield 24 triangles.
1 strip, 5¼" x 42"; crosscut into 6 squares, 5¼" x 5¼".
    Cut each square into quarters diagonally to yield
    24 triangles.
6 strips, 5½" x 42"

From the large-scale print, cut:
1 strip, 3⅜" x 42"; crosscut into 6 squares, 3⅜" x 3⅜"
2 strips, 8½" x 42"; crosscut into 6 squares, 8½" x 8½"

Piecing Block A

1. Sew each pink 4⅛" triangle to a black 4⅛" triangle along the short edges to make a pieced triangle. Press the seam allowances toward the black triangles. Sew two pieced triangles together to make an hourglass unit. Press the seam allowance in either direction. Repeat to make a total of 24 units.

Make 24.

2. Sew a star print 2⅞" triangle to one side of each star print square. Press the seam allowances toward the squares.

Make 24.

3. Sew an hourglass unit from step 1 to each unit from step 2. Press the seam allowances toward the squares.

Make 24.

4. Lay out four units from step 3, four pink 9¼" triangles, and one large-scale print 3⅜" square into diagonal rows. Sew the pieces in each row together. Press the seam allowances in the directions indicated. Sew the rows together. Press the seam allowances toward the outer rows. Repeat to make a total of six blocks.

Block A.
Make 6.

Piecing Block B

1. Sew pink 5¼" triangles to each side of a star print 5¼" triangle. Press the seam allowances toward the pink triangles. Repeat to make a total of 24 units.

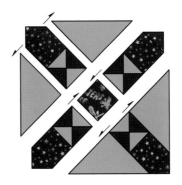

Make 24.

2. Sew two units from step 1 to opposite sides of a large-scale 8½" square. Press the seam allowances away from the square. Repeat on the remaining two sides. Repeat to make a total of six units.

Make 6.

3. Sew a star print 4⅞" triangle to the corners of each unit from step 2. Press the seam allowances toward the star print triangles.

Block B.
Make 6.

Assembling the Quilt Top

1. Refer to the quilt assembly diagram to lay out the blocks into four rows of three blocks each, alternating the blocks in each row and from row to row. Sew the blocks in each row together. Press the seam allowances in opposite directions from row to row. Sew the rows together. Press the seam allowances in one direction.
2. Use the black 1"-wide strips and refer to "Borders" on page 12 to apply the inner border to the quilt top using the butted-corners technique. Repeat for the outer border, using the star print 5½"-wide strips.

Quilting and Binding

1. Refer to "Preparing the Quilt Sandwich" on page 13 to layer the quilt top, batting, and backing.
2. Hand or machine quilt as desired.
3. Refer to "Binding" on page 14 to bind the quilt edges with the black 2"-wide strips.

Quilting Suggestion

This quilt is one in which an allover quilting pattern would work well. However, because I didn't want to detract from the themed fabric, I simply outline quilted all the pink triangles and the theme-fabric squares. A stars-and-loops meandering design in the border complements the star print fabric.

Quilt assembly

Pieced and quilted by Karen Sievert

The alternate patterns created by the joining of the two blocks in this quilt are so intriguing. Sometimes I see large circles, sometimes I see stars, and sometimes I see medallions. It's one of those neat little tricks of the eye! With 15" blocks, even a queen-size quilt stitches up quickly.

Finished quilt: 90½" x 105½"
Finished block: 15" x 15"

Materials

Yardages are based on 42"-wide fabric unless otherwise indicated.

5¼ yards of paisley print for blocks, outer border, and binding
3⅛ yards of navy fabric for blocks and inner border
2⅓ yards of light green fabric for blocks
2¼ yards of light blue fabric for blocks
3¼ yards of 108"-wide fabric for backing
98" x 113" piece of batting

Cutting

All measurements include ¼"-wide seam allowances.

From the light green fabric, cut:
10 strips, 5⅞" x 42"; crosscut into 60 squares, 5⅞" x 5⅞"
3 strips, 5½" x 42"; crosscut into 15 squares, 5½" x 5½"

From the navy fabric, cut:
10 strips, 5⅞" x 42"; crosscut into 60 squares, 5⅞" x 5⅞"
3 strips, 6¼" x 42"; crosscut into 15 squares, 6¼" x 6¼".
   Cut each square into quarters diagonally to yield 60 triangles.
9 strips, 2" x 42"

From the paisley print, cut:
3 strips, 3" x 42"
10 strips, 5⅞" x 42"; crosscut into 60 squares, 5⅞" x 5⅞"
3 strips, 6¼" x 42"; crosscut into 15 squares, 6¼" x 6¼".
   Cut each square into quarters diagonally to yield 60 triangles.
10 strips, 6½" x 42"
10 strips, 2" x 42"

From the light blue fabric, cut:
3 strips, 3" x 42"
10 strips, 6¼" x 42"; crosscut into:
   60 rectangles, 6¼" x 3⅛"
   30 squares, 6¼" x 6¼"; cut each square into quarters diagonally to yield 120 triangles

Piecing Block A

1. Draw a diagonal line from corner to corner on the wrong side of each light green 5⅞" square. With the marked squares on top, layer each square with a navy 5⅞" square, right sides together. Stitch ¼" away from both sides of the drawn line. Cut the squares apart on the line to yield 120 half-square-triangle units. Press the seam allowances toward the navy triangles. Trim the dog-ears. Set aside 60 units for block B.

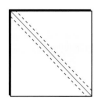
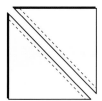

Make 120.

2. Mark the center point on the top edge of each paisley 5⅞" square. Cut from the bottom corners to the mark on each square to make a triangle.

Make 60.

3. Place two light blue rectangles right sides together. Cut diagonally from corner to corner. You will have two right-side triangles and two left-side triangles. Repeat with the remaining rectangles to make 60 right-side triangles and 60 left-side triangles.

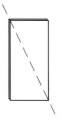

Left-side triangle. Make 60. Right-side triangle. Make 60.

4. Lay out one light blue left-side triangle, one light blue right-side triangle, and one paisley triangle as shown. Sew the left-side triangle to the left edge of the paisley triangle, matching the tips at the paisley triangle point. Press the seam allowance toward the light blue triangle. Add the right-side triangle to the right edge in the same manner. Repeat to make a total of 60 units. Trim the dog-ears.

Match tips.

Make 60.

5. With right sides together, sew a light blue 3" x 42" strip to a paisley 3" x 42" strip along one long edge to make a strip set. Repeat to make a total of three strip sets. Press the seam allowances toward the paisley strips. Crosscut the strip sets into 30 segments, 3" wide.

3"

Make 3 strip sets.
Cut 30 segments.

6. Sew two segments together to make a four-patch unit. Repeat to make a total of 15 units.

Make 15.

7. Lay out four half-square-triangle units from step 1, four triangle units from step 4, and one four-patch unit from step 6 into three horizontal rows. Sew the units in each row together. Press the seam allowances in the directions indicated. Sew the rows together. Press the seam allowances toward the middle row. Repeat to make a total of 15 blocks.

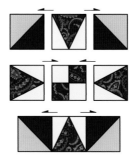 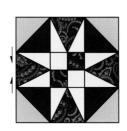

Block A.
Make 15.

Piecing Block B

1. Using the 6¼" triangles, lay out one paisley triangle, one navy triangle, and two light blue triangles as shown. Sew the triangles into pairs. Press the seam allowances away from the light blue triangles. Sew the pairs together to make an hourglass unit. Press the seam allowance toward the paisley half. Repeat to make a total of 60 units.

Make 60.

2. Lay out four half-square-triangle units that you set aside from step 1 of "Piecing Block A," four hour-glass units from step 1, and one light green 5½ square into three horizontal rows. Sew the pieces in each row together. Press the seam allowances in the directions indicated. Sew the rows together. Press the seam allowances toward the middle row. Repeat to make a total of 15 blocks.

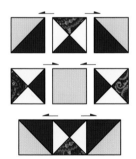 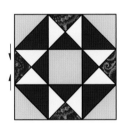

Block B.
Make 15.

Assembling the Quilt Top

1. Refer to the quilt assembly diagram to lay out the blocks in six rows of five blocks each, alternating the blocks in each row and from row to row. Sew the blocks in each row together. Rotate the blocks as needed so the seam allowances oppose each other. Press the seam allowances in opposite directions from row to row. Sew the rows together. Press the seam allowances in one direction.

2. Use the navy 2"-wide strips and refer to "Borders" on page 12 to apply the inner border to the quilt top using the butted-corners technique. Repeat for the outer border using the paisley 6½"-wide strips.

Quilt assembly

Quilting and Binding

1. Refer to "Preparing the Quilt Sandwich" on page 13 to layer the quilt top, batting, and backing.
2. Hand or machine quilt as desired.
3. Refer to "Binding" on page 14 to bind the quilt edges with the paisley 2"-wide strips.

Quilting Suggestion

You have endless quilting possibilities for this quilt. I outline quilted all the light blue areas, put freehand feathers in the large and small light green spaces, and outline quilted and echo quilted the paisley and navy fabrics.

Stacie's Quilt

Pieced and quilted by Karen Sievert

A quilt is one of the very best gifts we can give to another person. Before I started sewing, someone gave me a baby quilt for my son Wayne. At the time, I was not a quilter, and I was blown away that someone would take the time and effort to make something so beautiful, and then give it away! I can assure you, I treasure that memory and that quilt. This quilt was made for my best friend's daughter on the occasion of her marriage. My hope is that she'll treasure this quilt as much as I treasure the first quilt given to me!

Finished quilt: 81½" x 97½"
Finished block: 16" x 16"

Materials

Yardages are based on 42"-wide fabric unless otherwise indicated.

4 yards of black fabric for blocks, outer border, and binding
1¾ yards of white fabric for blocks
1½ yards of off-white fabric for blocks
1⅓ yards of large-scale floral for block A
1 yard of burgundy fabric for block B and inner border
⅞ yard of green fabric for block B
2½ yards of 108"-wide fabric for backing
89" x 105" piece of batting

Cutting

All measurements include ¼"-wide seam allowances.

From the off-white fabric, cut:
5 strips, 4⅞" x 42"; crosscut into 40 squares, 4⅞" x 4⅞".
    Cut 20 squares in half diagonally to yield 40 triangles.
5 strips, 4½" x 42"; crosscut into 40 squares, 4½" x 4½"

From the black fabric, cut:
3 strips, 4⅞" x 42"; crosscut into 20 squares, 4⅞" x 4⅞"
5 strips, 3⅜" x 42"; crosscut into 50 squares, 3⅜" x 3⅜"
2 strips, 1⅞" x 42"; crosscut into 40 squares, 1⅞" x 1⅞"
9 strips, 8½" x 42"
10 strips, 2" x 42"

From the white fabric, cut:
5 strips, 4⅞" x 42"; crosscut into 40 squares, 4⅞" x 4⅞".
    Cut each square in half diagonally to yield 80 triangles.
3 strips, 5¼" x 42"; crosscut into 20 squares, 5¼" x 5¼".
    Cut each square into quarters diagonally to yield
    80 triangles.
5 strips, 2⅞" x 42"; crosscut into 60 squares, 2⅞" x 2⅞".
    Cut each square in half diagonally to yield 120 triangles.

From the large-scale floral, cut:
2 strips, 6⅛" x 42"; crosscut into 10 squares, 6⅛" x 6⅛"
3 strips, 9¼" x 42"; crosscut into 10 squares, 9¼" x 9 ¼".
    Cut each square into quarters diagonally to yield 40
    triangles.

From the burgundy fabric, cut:
3 strips, 2½" x 42"; crosscut into 40 squares, 2½" x 2½"
3 strips, 2⅞" x 42"; crosscut into 40 squares, 2⅞" x 2⅞".
    Cut each square in half diagonally to yield 80 triangles.
2 strips, 3¼" x 42"; crosscut into 20 squares, 3¼" x 3¼".
    Cut each square into quarters diagonally to yield
    80 triangles.
8 strips, 1" x 42"

From the green fabric, cut:
10 strips, 2½" x 42"; crosscut into 80 rectangles, 2½" x 4⅞"

Piecing Block A

1. Draw a diagonal line from corner to corner on the wrong sides of each off-white 4⅞" square. With the marked squares on top, layer each square with a black 4⅞" square, right sides together. Stitch ¼" away from both sides of the drawn line. Cut the squares apart on the line to yield 40 half-square-triangle units. Press the seam allowances toward the black triangles. Trim the dog-ears.

Make 40.

2. Sew two white 4⅞" triangles to a large-scale floral 9¼" triangle, pressing toward the white triangles after each addition. Repeat to make a total of 40 flying-geese units.

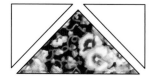 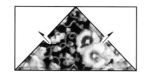

Make 40.

3. Sew off-white triangles to opposite sides of a large-scale floral 6⅛" square. Press the seam allowances toward the off-white triangles. Repeat for the remaining two sides. Repeat to make a total of 10 center units.

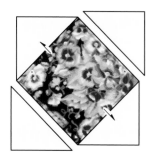 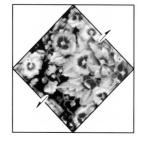

Make 10.

4. Lay out four half-square-triangle units from step 1, four flying-geese units from step 2, and one center unit from step 3 into three horizontal rows. Sew the units in each row together. Press the seam allowances in the directions indicated. Sew the rows together. Press the seam allowances toward the outer rows. Repeat to make a total of 10 blocks.

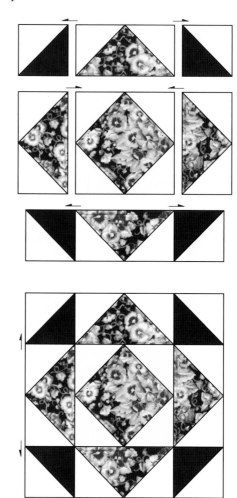

Block A.
Make 10.

Piecing Block B

1. Sew white 2⅞" triangles to opposite sides of a black 3⅜" square. Press the seam allowances toward the white triangles. Repeat for the remaining two sides. Repeat to make a total of 10 units.

Make 10.

2. Sew burgundy 3¼" triangles to two adjacent sides of a black 1⅞" square. Press the seam allowances toward the burgundy triangles. Repeat to make a total of 40 units.

Make 40.

3. Sew white 2⅞" triangles to the short edges of each unit from step 2. Press the seam allowances toward the white triangles.

Make 40.

4. Lay out one unit from step 1, four units from step 3, and four burgundy 2½" squares into three horizontal rows. Sew the pieces in each row together. Press the seam allowances in the directions indicated. Sew the rows together. Press the seam allowances toward the center row. Repeat to make a total of 10 center units.

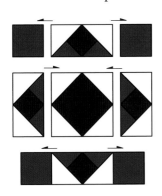

Make 10.

5. Layer two green rectangles right sides together. Align the 45° angle of your ruler with the bottom edge of the rectangles. Cut along the right edge of the ruler to make two trapezoids. Repeat with the remaining rectangles. Separate the trapezoids into 40 left-side trapezoids and 40 right-side trapezoids.

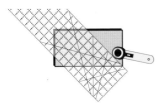

Left-side trapezoid. Make 40.   Right-side trapezoid. Make 40.

6. Sew a burgundy 2⅞" triangle to each of the green trapezoids as shown to make 40 left units and 40 right units. Press the seam allowances toward the burgundy triangles.

Make 40.

Make 40.

7. Sew white 5¼" triangles to two adjacent sides of a black 3⅜" square. Press the seam allowances toward the white triangles. Repeat to make a total of 40 units.

Make 40.

8. Sew one left and one right trapezoid unit to each unit from step 7. Press the seam allowances toward the trapezoid units.

Make 40.

9. Lay out one center unit from step 4, four units from step 8, and four off-white 4½" squares into three horizontal rows. Sew the pieces in each row together. Press the seam allowances in the directions indicated. Sew the rows together. Press the seam allowances toward the outer rows. Repeat to make a total of 10 blocks.

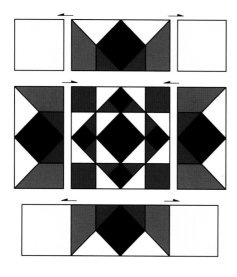

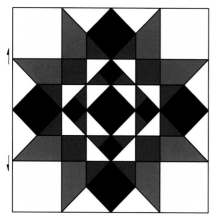

Block B.
Make 10.

Assembling the Quilt Top

1. Refer to the quilt assembly diagram to lay out the blocks into five rows of four blocks each, alternating the blocks in each row and from row to row. Rotate the blocks as needed so the seam allowances oppose each other. Sew the blocks in each row together. Press the seam allowances in opposite directions from row to row. Sew the rows together. Press the seam allowances in one direction.

2. Use the burgundy 1"-wide strips and refer to "Borders" on page 12 to apply the inner border to the quilt top using the butted-corners technique. Repeat for the outer border using the black 8½"-wide strips.

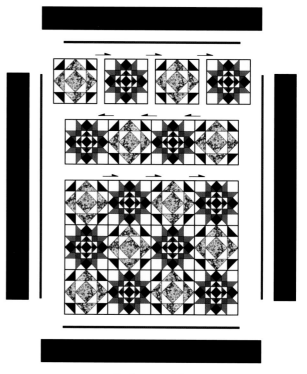

Quilt assembly

Quilting and Binding

1. Refer to "Preparing the Quilt Sandwich" on page 13 to layer the quilt top, batting, and backing.
2. Hand or machine quilt as desired.
3. Refer to "Binding" on page 14 to bind the quilt edges with the black 2"-wide strips.

Quilting Suggestion

This quilt can be quilted quite simply. I outline quilted the black and large floral pieces, put a leaf in each of the green pieces, channel quilted the frames around the square-in-a-square units of the block centers, and stitched a freehand feather in the off-white prisms. A curling feather in the border complements the feathers in the off-white prisms.

Victorian Nights

Finished quilt: 96½" x 112½"

This quilt, made by Karen Sievert and quilted by Monica Forsyth, is a wonderful example of how very different the same quilt can look with different fabric choices. It's made using the same pattern as "Stacie's Quilt," but fabrics were chosen to create a more blended look. Notice how the small-scale floral and paisley prints give this particular quilt a Victorian flair.

About the Author

Karen began her quiltmaking journey in 1997 when her sister, Barbara, dragged her into a quilt shop, firmly stating that she needed a hobby! Immediately hooked, Karen has been quilting, designing, and teaching ever since. She is the past owner of two quilt shops and now owns her own long-arm quilting business.

An award-winning quilter, Karen states that what she loves most about quilting is the friendships she's formed with other quilters: friendships that have sustained her through the many moves she's made due to her husband's military career.

Karen was born in Kwajalein in the Marshall Islands and currently resides in Gainesville, Virginia, with her husband, Vince, and her three children, Wayne, Shannah, and Travis.

There's More Online!

⊛ **Karen's blog.** Find it at www.theniftyneedle.blogspot.com. "Quilting-related commentary, patterns, and pictures. Daily life, family and friends, recipes to share."

⊛ **The Nifty Needle website.** To see more of Karen Sievert's designs and find tips related to long-arm machine quilting, go to www.theniftyneedle.com.

⊛ **Martingale & Company/That Patchwork Place®.** For more great books on quilting, knitting, crochet, and more, visit www.martingale-pub.com.

New and Best-Selling Titles from

That Patchwork Place®   America's Best-Loved
Quilt Books®

Martingale® & COMPANY

America's Best-Loved Craft & Hobby Books®
America's Best-Loved Knitting Books®

APPLIQUÉ
Appliqué Quilt Revival
Beautiful Blooms
Cutting-Garden Quilts
Dream Landscapes
Easy Appliqué Blocks
Simple Comforts
Sunbonnet Sue and Scottie Too

BABIES AND CHILDREN
Baby's First Quilts
Let's Pretend
Snuggle-and-Learn Quilts for Kids
Sweet and Simple Baby Quilts
Warm Welcome—NEW!

BEGINNER
Color for the Terrified Quilter
Four-Patch Frolic—NEW!
Happy Endings, Revised Edition
Machine Appliqué for the Terrified Quilter
Quilting Your Style—NEW!
Your First Quilt Book (or it should be!)

GENERAL QUILTMAKING
American Jane's Quilts for All Seasons
Bits and Pieces
Bold and Beautiful
Country-Fresh Quilts
Creating Your Perfect Quilting Space
Fat-Quarter Quilting—NEW!
Fig Tree Quilts: Fresh Vintage Sewing
Folk-Art Favorites
Follow-the-Line Quilting Designs
  Volume Three
Gathered from the Garden
The New Handmade
Points of View
Prairie Children and Their Quilts
Quilt Challenge—NEW!
Quilt Revival
A Quilter's Diary
Quilter's Happy Hour

Quilting for Joy
Quilts from Paradise—NEW!
Remembering Adelia
Simple Seasons
Skinny Quilts and Table Runners
Twice Quilted

HOLIDAY AND SEASONAL
Candy Cane Lane—NEW!
Christmas Quilts from Hopscotch
Comfort and Joy
Deck the Halls—NEW!
Holiday Wrappings

HOOKED RUGS, NEEDLE FELTING, AND PUNCHNEEDLE
Miniature Punchneedle Embroidery
Needle Felting with Cotton and Wool
Needle-Felting Magic

PAPER PIECING
A Year of Paper Piecing
Easy Reversible Vests, Revised Edition
Paper-Pieced Mini Quilts
Show Me How to Paper Piece

PIECING
501 Rotary-Cut Quilt Blocks
Favorite Traditional Quilts Made Easy
Loose Change
Mosaic Picture Quilts
New Cuts for New Quilts
On-Point Quilts
Ribbon Star Quilts
Rolling Along

QUICK QUILTS
40 Fabulous Quick-Cut Quilts
Charmed, I'm Sure—NEW!
Instant Bargello
Quilts on the Double
Sew Fun, Sew Colorful Quilts
Supersize 'Em!

SCRAP QUILTS
Nickel Quilts
Save the Scraps
Scrap-Basket Surprises
Simple Strategies for Scrap Quilts

CRAFTS
A to Z of Sewing
Art from the Heart
The Beader's Handbook
Dolly Mama Beads
Embellished Memories
Friendship Bracelets All Grown Up
Making Beautiful Jewelry
Paper It!
Trading Card Treasures

KNITTING & CROCHET
365 Crochet Stitches a Year
365 Knitting Stitches a Year
A to Z of Knitting
All about Crochet—NEW!
All about Knitting
Amigurumi World
Amigurumi Two!—NEW!
Beyond Wool
Cable Confidence
Casual, Elegant Knits
Crocheted Pursenalities
Knitted Finger Puppets
The Knitter's Book of Finishing
  Techniques
Knitting Circles around Socks
*Knitting More Circles around
  Socks—NEW!*
Knits from the North Sea—NEW!
More Sensational Knitted Socks
*New Twists on Twined Knitting—
  NEW!*
Pursenalities
Simple Stitches
Toe-Up Techniques for Hand-
  Knit Socks, Revised Edition
Together or Separate

Our books are available at bookstores and your favorite craft, fabric, and yarn retailers. If you don't see the title you're looking for, visit us at **www.martingale-pub.com** or contact us at:

1-800-426-3126
International: 1-425-483-3313
Fax: 1-425-486-7596 • Email: info@martingale-pub.com